Seminar: Race & the Law

A Better Police Force: Lessons from the Classroom

A Proposal by

Haneefah Khaaliq[1]

---

[1] Haneefah Khaaliq is a third year law student at Valparaiso University School of Law. She is an intern for the City of Gary Mayor Karen Freeman-Wilson. She is from Chicago, Illinois and has interests in education, politics and law. She wishes to thank Professor Mary Szto of the Valparaiso University Law School Faculty Community for her sincere dedication in inspiring students in Seminar: Race and the Law Class of 2017.

Table of Contents

I. INTRODUCTION

The following proposal was inspired by the invitation to present at Valparaiso University's Annual Martin Luther King Jr. Celebration in 2017. For more than 25 years the Valparaiso University community has gathered to collectively reflect on the life and legacy of Dr. King.

The purpose of this proposal is to catalyze a greater dialogue about harmony between the community and law enforcement agencies. First I will discuss the origin of the police force and discuss today's police training and the "warrior mindset" which is detrimental to community policing. I then ask: What makes a better police force? I then share my experiences as a former teacher and the challenges I faced in creating a better classroom. Although comparing a classroom to the police force may seem unusual, I encourage readers to consider that both are groups of individuals who can be shaped and molded into their full potential.

I then provide the techniques that made a better classroom and demonstrate how these same techniques can be combined and applied to the police force to create a better and stronger law enforcement agency. My proposal ends encouragingly with a quote from Dr. King for all races and classes of people.

II. THE ORIGINS OF THE POLICE FORCE

The origin of the police force in the United States followed the development of the police force in England.[2] The U.S.'s first police force was composed of community volunteers who

---

[2] Dr. Gary Potter,*The History of Policing in the United States, Part 1*, Eastern Kentucky University Police Studies Online (Feb. 27, 2017, 6:00 PM), http://plsonline.eku.edu/insidelook/history-policing-united-states-part-1.

warned of impending dangers.[3] In the Northern United States, Boston was the first city in 1635 to create a night watch, followed by New York in 1658 and Philadelphia in 1700. [4] Boston was also the first city to establish a substantial police force, followed by New York in 1845 and Chicago in 1851. [5] By the 1880s all United States cities had a municipal police force.[6] In the Southern states, however, the formation of American policing took on a different form and purpose.[7] The beginnings of police organizations in the South began with "slave patrols."[8] Slave patrols had three primary duties: (1) to return runaway slaves; (2) to deter slave revolts; and (3) to discipline slave-workers.[9] After the Civil War, the slave patrols evolved into Southern police departments as a means of regulating freed slaves who were agricultural workers.[10] As time progressed, these police departments were used to enforce "Jim Crow" segregation laws and generally controlled African-Americans rights and access to the political process.[11]

All over the United States, modern police forces had evolved into respondents to disorder; however, what constituted as "disorder" was largely dependent upon who defined the term.[12] In the 19th century America, disorder was largely defined by mercantile interests.[13] As the population rose, these commercial or economic interests seemed to have a great interest in

---

[3] *Id.*
[4] *Id.*
[5] *Id.*
[6] *Id.*
[7] *Id.*
[8] Platt, Tony, *Crime and Punishment in the United States: Immediate and Long-Term Reforms from a Marxist Perspective*, Crime and Social Justice 18 (1982).
[9] Potter, *supra.*
[10] *Id.*
[11] *Id.*
[12]
[13] *Id.*

controlling people rather than controlling crime.[14] Maintaining a workforce for factory

production and ensuring a tranquil community for the advancement of commerce required social

control and was achieved by using a police force.[15] Social control was accomplished by

guilefully defining it as crime control and raising the apparition of a dangerous class.[16] This

"dangerous class" was easily identifiable because it consisted of the poor, free blacks, and

immigrants.[17] This isolation of dangerous individuals created much of the focus in crime control

we have today.[18] This also created early American police departments that were notoriously

corrupt and cruel to the so called dangerous class.[19]

The modern U.S. police force completely altered the original purpose for having police.[20]

Originally, policing was a reactive endeavor only occurring in response to a specific crime;

however, it wasn't long before police were being used to also *prevent* crime and that meant

police insertion into our everyday lives.[21] This was a previously unknown concept in both

England and the U.S.[22]

In 1967, during the era of the Civil Rights Movement, in an effort to professionalize the

police force and reduce corruption, President Lyndon B. Johnson appointed nineteen people to

---

[14] *Id.*
[15] *Id.*
[16] *Id.*
[17] Lundman, Robert J., *Police and Policing: An Introduction*, New York, New York: Holt, Rinehart & Winston, (1980).
[18] *Id.*
[19] Potter, *supra.*
[20] *Id.*
[21] Parks, Evelyn, *From Constabulary to Police Society: Implications for Social Control*, In Whose Law? What Order?, edited by William Chambliss and Michael Mankoff, New York, New York: Wiley (1976).
[22] *Id.*

study the criminal justice system.[23] In regards to the appointment, President Johnson stated there was no agency of government in American history that had undertaken to probe so fully and deeply into the problems of American crime and policing.[24] President Johnson assigned the nineteen individuals with the responsibility of repairing the police system.[25] After the report was issued in 1967, it laid out reorganization plans for police departments across America that would now require police training.[26]

III. THE WARRIOR MINDSET

Unfortunately, the required training lacked specifics and evolved into officers being trained to have what is known as the "warrior mindset."[27] In fact, today's police training has become so attached to the warrior concept that at some law enforcement agencies, it has become normal to refer to one's fellow officer as a "warrior."[28] Although referring to each other as warriors may have good intentions, it creates obstacles to improving relations between the police and the community.[29] The reason is because the warrior mindset means survival no matter what conditions exist; it means never giving up or giving in and refers to the attitude that officers, like soldiers, should have a commitment to survive any situation they believe to be bad.[30] In the first

---

[23]Johnson, Lyndon B. *(March 8, 1965). "Special Message to the Congress on Law Enforcement and the Administration of Justice". Retrieved April 3, 2013.*
[24] *Id.*
[25] *Id.*
[26] Dempsey, John S. and Forst, Linda S. *(2011). An Introduction to Policing. Cengage Learning. p. 80. ISBN 978-1-111-13772-4. Retrieved April 3, 2013 – via Google Books.*
[27] Seth Stoughton, Comment, Law Enforcement's 'Warrior' Problem, 128 Harv. L. Rev. F. 225 (2015), *available at http://harvardlawreview.org/2015/04/law-enforcements-warrior-problem.*
[28] *Id.*
[29] *Id.*
[30] *Id.*

days of police training, cadets are told that their prime concern and first rule of law is to return home at the end of their shift, but that they are living in a hostile world that wants to prevent it.[31] They are told that death is constantly one misstep away.[32] Training materials at the New Mexico Police Academy inform recruits that suspects are prepared to react violently and that they (the police) can die "today, tomorrow, or next Friday."[33]

Under this type of cognition, officers are subconsciously and undoubtedly engaged in combat with every person they come in contact with.[34] Officers do not only learn to be cautious and vigilant but, are trained to fear the worst, and as a result, they are highly suspicious and on alert at all times.[35] Recruits are not only told that they should be afraid in training but, also informally from supervisors and more experienced officers that fear and hypervigilance is the key to survival.[36] A recent police article states: "Remain humble and compassionate; be professional and courteous—and have a plan to kill everyone you meet."[37] This approach to policing creates a barrier to true community policing and invites tension.[38] On the contrary, community policing involves establishing trust and building relationships with the people of a

---

[31] *Id.*

[32] *Id.*

[33] *Uriel J. Garcia, Experts Say Strongly Worded Police Curriculum Is Risky with Cadets, Santa Fe New Mexican (Mar. 25, 2014), http://www.santafenewmexican.com/news/local_news/experts-say-strongly-worded-police-curriculum-is-risky-with-cadets/article_6fcb7d45-436c-5e48-aa06-2fc6fdcc35a1.html [http://perma.cc/FBQ2-LYTP].*

[34] Stoughton, *supra.*

[35] *Id.*

[36] *Id.*

[37] *John Bennett, How Command Presence Affects Your Survival, PoliceOne.com (Oct. 7, 2010), http://www.policeone.com/Officer-Safety/articles/2748139-How-command-presence-affects-your-survival [http://perma.cc/CKF3-Y8C6].*

[38] Stoughton, *supra.*

community.[39] How can police help build communities when they are trained to fear them? The warrior mentality makes policing dangerous for both officers and civilians by cultivating hostility.[40] For these reasons, as a society, we must ask ourselves what makes a better police force for communities and how can we provide our police with training that improves community relations instead of destroying them before they have a chance?

IV. A BETTER CLASSROOM, A BETTER POLICE FORCE

As a former educator, when asked what makes a better police force I automatically think of what makes a better classroom. Forgive me. Of course, I'm aware of how odd this may sound. The responsibilities of police officers do not compare with those given to say, for example, a group of sixth graders. It would be impractical to reduce the authority given to police officers and compare their assignments with those given to students. I've never been involved with the police, so I can only imagine what skills and dedication one must have to be a part of an agency where everyday individuals sacrifice their lives for the greater good. However, from 2006-2010, I was a public school teacher. Needless to say, the job was extremely challenging but, through mistakes, hard work and dedication, I became accustomed to receiving awards for my students' academic achievement and was praised by my principals for running what you would call a "tight ship." I admit I was a strict and demanding school teacher who required all students to perform well. Failure was not an option in my classroom, and that was my reputation. My students were known for their achievements because I required them. Many of them not only

---

[39] *Id.*
[40] *Id.*

passed my classroom tests, but school and state-wide tests, often passing and earning extra points on them. As you can see, to this day, I pride myself on their accomplishments.

In the school year 2009-2010, little did I know, I was going to be presented with one of my greatest challenges yet: teaching the most difficult sixth grade classroom in the entire school district. This will all come together in a moment so, bare with me. The classroom's reputation was so bad I had to be escorted by the principal and school security just to preview it. Standing in the doorway, I could not believe my eyes. I had never seen such disarray in all my life. As the third or fourth substitute teacher that week struggled to keep the attention of two students in the front of the room, five or six students were sprawled across the floor in the back part of the room and appeared to be napping. As I entered, the principal shared with me that three teachers had already been introduced to the classroom and quit the next day. I looked on as two or three more students were on their cellular phones. A few of them were coloring or drawing or looking out the window. Others were gathered around one computer taking turns playing a computer game that from what I could see had absolutely nothing to do with the lesson. The majority of them were absent. Meanwhile papers, pencils, and books were scattered everywhere across the floor. The classroom was in complete disorganization. As I continued to observe, I witnessed students snapping back at the substitute teacher and at each other. Further inquiry revealed even more shortcomings: not surprisingly, out of the three sixth grade classrooms in the entire school, this class performed the absolute worst in both reading and math.

Why am I sharing this story with you? Today, we pose ourselves with a question: What makes a better police force? I would dare to say that the answer lies in the same thing that makes a better classroom. Allow me to explain. After taking over the classroom in becoming the new sixth grade teacher, I am proud to say that, in less than three months time, the very same classroom I observed, the very classroom that was in such disorder and disarray, was now a completely transformed classroom. In less than three months time, the students were not only respectful, but highly achieving and outperforming the other two sixth grade classrooms in the school. They were measuring up to the accomplishments of other sixth graders throughout the school district. The question is: how was it done?

As stated before, comparing the police force to a classroom is unusual. That is not the point of this proposal. The authority, power, and responsibilities given to police do not compare with that of sixth graders. We absolutely respect the police. We absolutely honor them and are grateful for what they do. But both students and police officers can be molded and shaped into their full potential. What I was given was a broken classroom that was restructured and redesigned to meet the needs of the school community. I believe that any police force that finds itself broken can be restructured and redesigned in the same way to meet the overall needs of the community.

V. **THE SEVEN TECHNIQUES TO A BETTER FORCE**

Today, our society has witnessed what some would opine as a complete breakdown of our police force just as this classroom was. The only persons who believe the force is doing well may be the ones whose lives have not yet been negatively impacted. Many people across this nation are scared to death of the police just as most teachers were of the students in that classroom. But this is not a time to be scared. It is a time to require a better police force. Now more than ever, the national dialogue needs to change about what is needed to make that happen. So, I return to the question that was presented earlier: how exactly was it done? Can these techniques be used to make a better police force?

A. DISCIPLINE AND MANAGEMENT

What made this classroom better shall be no secret. The first technique I used was to establish classroom management through a consistent discipline policy. This held each student accountable and set clear boundaries for behavior. Effective classroom management decreases student misbehavior and increases time students spend learning.[41] Effective classroom management strategies prevent problems in the classroom and promote a positive learning environment.[42] They also work by creating an orderly learning environment and emphasizing student expectations for behavior and success.[43] In the same way, police need management and discipline to deter police misbehavior and corruption.[44]

Former New York Police Commissioner William Joseph Bratton is experienced in disciplining police having spent several years combined as Chief of the Los Angeles Police Department and Commissioner of the Boston Police Department.[45] Although he stepped down

---

[41] American Psychological Association, Section on Education and Psychology: Pre-K to 12 Education, Classroom Management, http://www.apa.org/education/k12/classroom-mgmt.aspx,(last visited February 28, 2017).
[42] *Id.*
[43] *Id.*
[44]Bratton, Bill *(14 August 2011)*. *"American 'super cop' called in by Cameron reveals how to halt the hoodlums: 'I don't do it… but I can tell you how to hit gangs'"*. *Daily Mail. London.*
[45] William Bratton, https://en.wikipedia.org/w/index.php?title=William_Bratton&oldid=773094832 (last visited Apr. 3, 2017).

shortly after his appointment in 2014, he strived to give his commanders more authority in deciding how to punish police officers for misconduct.[46] Studies show that when little to no boundaries or rules have been set or adhered to, those who are given authoritative power tend to abuse it.[47] Therefore, a consistent discipline policy is necessary to ensure that police officers remain in order and functional.[48] Police departments must make it clear that certain police behaviors will not be tolerated.[49]

B. NEW LEARNING EXPERIENCES

The second technique I used in the classroom was to improve students' learning experiences outside of what was expected. For example, instead of giving students a few pages to read at night for homework, I scheduled field trips and invited guest speakers to come in. Most of all, I allowed students to learn through play, experimentation, and creation. Play allows students to develop their own imagination and creativity while improving their own cognitive, emotional, and physical strength.[50] It allows them to think for themselves and explore a world they can one day master.[51] It allows them to conquer their fears, practice adult roles, and develop

---

[46] Al Baker, *New York Police Shift Approach on Discipline,* New York Times, Sept. 21, 2015, at A1, *available at* https://www.nytimes.com/2015/09/21/nyregion/bratton-tries-a-community-policing-approach-on-the-new-york-police.html.

[47] Stanford prison experiment, https://en.wikipedia.org/w/index.php?title=Stanford_prison_experiment&oldid=766172183 (last visited Mar. 10, 2017).

[48] Baker, *supra.*

[49] *Id.*

[50] Kenneth Ginsburg, American Pediatrics Association, Section on Pediatrics: *The Importance of Play in Promoting Healthy Childhood Development and Maintaining Strong Parent-Child Bonds,* http://pediatrics.aappublications.org/content/119/1/182#xref-ref-4-1 (last visited March 1, 2017).

[51] *Id.*

new competencies that can lead to enhanced confidence and resiliency.[52] Resiliency will aid them when facing challenges in real life.[53] When play is controlled, learning is controlled and that means conformance to rules that ultimately hinder creativity, leadership, and group skills.[54] In this same way, our police need to be allowed to play in training. What? Did I just say that? Now is when I give the reader a moment to regain their composure because, I know how bizarre it sounds. Play training will allow police officers to conquer their fears and develop new competencies that will lead to an enhanced sense of self confidence, resiliency, and cognitive, emotional, and physical strength. So, what does play look like for police officers in regards to training?

As we all know, training is a vital component to the success of any law enforcement agency.[55] Law enforcement training can be divided into two categories: physical training and knowledge and skills based training.[56] I propose that play become an essential part of the knowledge and skills based training because it will allow officers the room to try out new ideas and to think outside the box of a traditional police response.[57] Allowing cadets to gain knowledge through play means allowing them to explore, ask questions, and be curious about their role; allowing them to be creative, to be given a chance to lead, and to work together to accomplish a goal or task without hindrances; allowing them to confront their fears and anxieties with

---

[52] *Id.*

[53] *Id.*

[54] *Id.*

[55] *Ed Flosi, Taking Training to the Next Level: Curriculum Development for Law Enforcement Pedagogy versus Andragogy, PoliceOne.com (Jun. 6, 2011), https://www.policeone.com/police-trainers/articles/3773478-Curriculum-development-for-law-enforcement-Pedagogy-versus-Andragogy.*

[56] *Id.*

[57] Terry Anderson, Every Officer is a Leader: Transforming Leadership in Police, Justice, and Public Safety (1989).

autonomy. While the "warrior mindset" tells officers what to think and why they should fear,[58] the proposed training provides officers with the tools and power they need to think for themselves and gives them the confidence to confront and ultimately extinguish their own fears. While the "warrior mindset" teaches officers to judge everyone as a suspect,[59] the proposed training will teach officers to make judgments only after a review of the totality of the circumstances with the use of such things as de-escalation tactics and good communication skills.[60] We will touch on the importance of good communication skills later.

C. MULTICULTURAL EDUCATION

The third technique I strived to use was creating classroom projects that created a multicultural education, which included the education of Europeans in America and the origins of the Americas. When students graduated from my classroom, they were well versed in the study of multiple religions, cultures, ethnicities, traditions, and persons with disabilities because I believed this would give them exposure to the world community. Multicultural education should not just be an add-on or an afterthought; classrooms everywhere should be infused with it in order to improve academic achievement and prepare students to be productive citizens of the society and world.[61] Multiculturalism in schools and local communities, along with domestic diversity and immigration has created a mixture of ethnicities and cultures in the United States.[62]

---

[58] Stoughton, *supra.*

[59] *Id.*

[60] *Id.*

[61] Geneva Gay, Association for Supervision and Curriculum Development, Section on Educational Leadership, 61(4), pp. 30-35), *The Importance of Multicultural Education*, (2004), http://pdo.ascd.org/lmscourses/PD11OC123/media/Diversity_Eff_Teaching_M1_Reading_Importance_of_Multicultural_Ed.pdf

[62] *Id.*

This calls for the development of programs and practices on all levels of education and in institutions that help learners respond positively and beneficially to diversity.[63] A century ago, W.E.B. Du Bois, an American sociologist,[64] proposed that the issue of the 20th century was conflict among racial groups.[65] Much has changed since Du Bois made this statement.[66] For example, laws against interracial marriages have been repealed and housing discrimination has been somewhat dismantled allowing people from different ethnic, racial, and cultural groups to live in close proximity of each other.[67] However, coexistence does not necessarily mean people are living in genuine communities where they care deeply for one another.[68] Therefore, multicultural education is essential to improving and preparing all students for the social, political, economic, and cultural fabric of the United States.[69] What would multicultural education look like in regards to police training?

Multicultural communities are a growing observable fact in the world and throughout America.[70] Due to a variety of factors, the world is now witnessing an increase in migration of large groups of people.[71] This movement has resulted in ethnic and cultural changes in communities all over the world.[72] These changes present a challenge for the criminal justice

---

[63] *Id.*

[64] W. E. B. Du Bois, https://en.wikipedia.org/w/index.php?title=W._E._B._Du_Bois&oldid=765858922 (last visited Mar. 2, 2017).

[65] Gay, *supra.*

[66] *Id.*

[67] *Id.*

[68] *Id.*

[69] *Id.*

[70] Journal of Police & Society: An Interdisciplinary Israeli Journal of Law Enforcement & Criminology, POLICING A MULTICULTURAL SOCIETY 1-249, (2003), https//www.ncjrs.gov/pdffiles1/nij/242329.pdf (last visited Mar 2017).

[71] *Id.*

[72] *Id.*

system and lawmakers.[73] For example, in some cultures, only females may be questioned by

other female police officers.[74] In other cultures, a male may only be questioned by other male

police officers.[75] These are just two examples, but keeping this in mind, one can easily observe

how communication can become distorted in regards to law enforcement when everyone is not

speaking the same language or the same background, values, and beliefs.[76] As one might

imagine, this miscommunication can lead to misunderstandings with law enforcement and

therefore, lead to unintended violence.[77] Failure to discuss the challenges police officers face in a

multicultural society and vice versa can lead to civil unrest and unnecessary violence.[78] In 2001,

The National Institute of Justice, together with the Israel National Police's Community & Civil

Guard Department held a meeting in Jerusalem, Israel to discuss multicultural education for

police officers in the United States and other countries that have a growing multicultural

community.[79] Amongst the things discussed was that policing in diverse neighborhoods is better

when the demographics of the neighborhood have been properly studied and given the utmost

consideration by police instead of ignoring them.[80] This means in order for police to be truly

effective in the neighborhoods they serve they must be allowed to study and assess them, which

allows them to then confront any biases they may hold. For example, in one study, it was

observed that police officers made distinctions between the ethical and moral character of

---

[73] *Id.*
[74] *Id.*
[75] *Id.*
[76] *Id.*
[77] *Id.*
[78] *Id.*
[79] *Id.*
[80] *Id.* at 135

residents living in low-income neighborhoods compared to residents living in middle-class neighborhoods.[81] These distinctions were consequential for how officers handled complaints.[82] In another study, a different group of police officers distinguished between anti-police and pro-police neighborhoods, again to a consequential effect.[83] Traffic stops in the anti-police neighborhoods took on a more hostile character.[84] Police must receive multicultural education in regards to their communities in order to be better prepared to serve in democratic societies.[85] Due to the overwhelming diversity of American cities, police must be trained in and knowledgeable of the idea that maintaining racial peace can be just as important, if not more important, than maintaining the enforcement of law.[86] Therefore, anyone who occupies the position of a police officer must be trained rigorously in multicultural awareness and the dangers of holding biases and prejudices. Furthermore, she must be continually observed and evaluated throughout her entire career to ensure that all citizens she comes in contact with have been treated with dignity and respect regardless of race, color, religion, sex, national origin, political affiliation, gender, gender identity, marital status, sexual orientation, ability, age, and any other factor upon which she may discriminate.

D. RESPECTFUL ENVIRONMENT

The fourth technique was to foster an environment of respect where all students felt respected. It is important that everyone is treated with respect in every classroom.[87] A classroom

---

[81] *Id.*
[82] *Id.*
[83] *Id.*
[84] *Id.*
[85] *Id.*
[86] *Id.* at 242
[87] Linda Tilton, STUDENT TO STUDENT RESPECT COVINGTON COVE PUBLICATIONS,

where respect is upheld fosters an environment where students feel it is safe to take risks, express opinions, and to genuinely be themselves.[88] Linda Tilton is an international author, speaker and K-12 teacher with over 30 years of experience in the field of education.[89] She believes that put downs diminish self-worth, discourage participation, build resentment, and suppress growth, learning, and curiosity.[90] Tilton also believes that sarcasm is equally as dangerous in the classroom as it attacks personal traits, qualities, and choices.[91] What does respect look like in law enforcement agencies?

In law enforcement agencies, respect is established by creating and maintaining a generally respectable work environment where officers feel it is safe to take risks, express their opinions, and genuinely be themselves. It is a place where officers are free from put downs and sarcasm; a place where they are not ridiculed or disrespected by anyone, no matter how high in the hierarchy the individual might be. It is a place where police are free to express their issues and concerns and know they will be taken seriously. I propose that when respect is upheld in the force, respect will be upheld in that force's community. Instead of being trained to have the "warrior mindset" police officers should be trained to have what is known as a "guardian mindset."[92] The guardian mindset places service above crime fighting and places the officer in a mental position as protector of the community instead of someone who fears the community.[93] In this way, the guardian mindset works to build respectable relationships with the public and

---

http://covingtoncove.com/student-to-student-respect/ (last visited Mar 2, 2017).
[88] *Id.*
[89] *Id.*
[90] *Id.*
[91] *Id.*
[92] Stoughton, *supra.*
[93] *Id.*

builds the kind of community policing our neighborhoods need.[94]

E. ATTENTION AND SUPPORT

The fifth technique I used was to give every student at one time or another, my absolute undivided attention and support. I made an effort to support each student through praise in hopes that it would improve their academic and behavioral performance. Each day I gave stickers, star awards, extra recess, candies, certificates, and other forms of extrinsic rewards to motivate students to perform well. Those students who didn't receive rewards were soon to turn their behavior around in an effort to be a part of the reward system. I balanced my reward system with intrinsic motivation by giving students verbal praise as often as I could for every single act or occurrence of good behavior and academic accomplishment. I made huge deals of the smallest acts of kindness performed by any student to ensure a feeling of appreciation. As a result, I began to notice that students developed a general liking for me and respected my efforts to make their school day pleasurable. In fact, I believe my reward system not only earned me respect amongst students, but popularity with faculty and staff members. Therefore, in regards to police, I propose that law enforcement agencies everywhere begin to find and implement ways to positively reinforce the good behavior of officers.

In regards to praise and motivation, Chief Jay Fortenbery, Ph.D., of Edenton, North Carolina, whose law enforcement experience spans nearly three decades,[95] calls attention to Abraham Maslow's motivational theory.[96] Based on Maslow's hierarchy of needs, after persons

---

[94] *Id.*

[95] Edenton Police Department, CHIEF OF POLICE, http://www.edentonpd.com/chiefofpolice.htm (last visited Mar 9, 2017).

[96] Jay Fortenbery, IMPROVING MOTIVATION AND PRODUCTIVITY OF POLICE OFFICERS THE FEDERAL BUREAU OF INVESTIGATION (2015),

obtain basic physiological essentials, such as food, water, shelter, safety, security, and a sense of belonging, they strive for praise and recognition for a job well-done.[97] This is followed by a desire for a fulfillment of one's talents and potentialities.[98] In studies dating back to the 1940s, recognition has outranked salary as a strong motivator.[99] Money is the extrinsic motivator for adults, while recognition and praise are intrinsic motivators.[100] When properly used, with reason and common sense, praise can be a powerful tool to motivate police officers.[101]

In addition to support through praise, I made an extreme effort to give each student at one time or another, my undivided attention, even if it was, at times, inconvenient. This was extremely important to me because I realized the more time I spent with students and/or their parents individually, the less time I spent disciplining them for misbehavior or dealing with academic failure. Therefore, I propose that, as apart of police ongoing growth and development, each police officer be encouraged to meet with trained individuals, detached from the law enforcement agency, for general check-ins, to have conversations with, and/or group discussions on how they are generally doing working on the force. It is important that these types of check-ins be inviting and understood by law enforcement officers to be confidential and safe. It is only by giving undivided attention to police through close communication that one can hope to make the best disposition[102] of them and to work through any barriers to efficiency.

---

https://leb.fbi.gov/2015/august/improving-motivation-and-productivity-of-police-officers (last visited Mar 9, 2017).

[97] *Id.*

[98] *Id.*

[99] *Id.*

[100] *Id.*

[101] *Id.*

[102] L. V. HARRISON & ROCHESTER BUREAU OF MUNICIPAL RESEARCH, REPORT ON A SURVEY OF THE POLICE BUREAU OF THE CITY OF ROCHESTER, N.Y.: SUBMITTED TO THE MAYOR, THE COMMISSIONER OF PUBLIC SAFETY AND THE CHIEF OF POLICE (2012).

F. HIGH EXPECTATIONS

The sixth technique I practiced daily was to change my overall expectation for my students. Assuming they didn't have it, I required a higher level of maturity and courtesy from each of them. By doing so, I encouraged them to think and act beyond what they were. For example, I found that if I treated my second graders as second graders then they only thought and acted as second graders. However, if I taught and treated them as third or even fourth grade students, then they began exhibiting characteristics of those in a higher grade. Many of them even began to understand some third and fourth grade concepts. While other second grade teachers struggled to keep the attention of their young learners, I had mastered it by requiring a higher level of maturity from each of my students. For example, I taught students why it was better to sit quietly and listen to adults rather than to run amuck and be loud and boisterous. I spent much time ingraining the importance of the golden rule of respect and why it was important to be able to do basic things, such as standing in line patiently or saying please and thank you. When I saw my students begin to act as older individuals, I introduced more complex lessons to them, such as times tables and division, and found that they were starting to understand. I was even able to carry on minimal conversations with them about what was happening in the local community and world news.

Applying the high expectation principle to the police force means not just claiming the existence of high expectations or assuming police officers have met them; but being clear about what the expectations are and how police will attain them. For example, I propose that law enforcement agencies everywhere try to refrain from expecting officers to be automatically equipped with certain skills, such as communication. Instead, law enforcement agencies should assume officers need further development and growth in areas like communication. Sergeant Andrew McCurdy of the King County Sheriff's Office Advanced Training Unit in Washington believes in setting high expectations for officers.[103] The King County Sheriff's Office uses procedural justice training as a way of setting clear expectations for how police should communicate and interact with each other and with the public.[104] Procedural justice training has four pillars that guide community policing in regards to communication: (1) giving people a voice in the process, (2) transparency in the decision-making process, (3) neutrality in the decision-making process, and (4) respecting a person's rights and dignity. Sergeant McCurdy goes a step further to suggest that officers should engage in setting expectations for themselves and that performance concerns should be addressed through student-centered training.[105] Sergeant McCurdy believes in building genuine relationships with people in the community he serves.[106] He currently runs his own after-school program and hopes to help build community relations through it.[107]

G. **EMPOWERMENT**

The seventh technique and final thing I practiced with my students, and perhaps the most

---

[103] Andrew McCurdy & Melissa Bradley, *Procedural Justice: High Expectations,* 6 COPS (2013), https://cops.usdoj.gov/html/dispatch/09-2013/procedural_justice_high_expectations.asp (last visited Mar 10, 2017).
[104] *Id.*
[105] *Id.*
[106] *Id.*
[107] Ted Land, WASHINGTON TEENS TEAM WITH POLICE FOR AFTERSCHOOL WORKOUTS KING 5 NEWS, KREM (2016), http://www.krem.com/news/local/northwest/wash-teens-team-with-police-for-afterschool-workouts/52815531 (last visited Mar 10, 2017).

important, was empowering them. I empowered students by entrusting each of them with responsibilities most teachers reserved for themselves. For example, I would take students who grasped concepts easily and use them to teach others at small group time. I noticed students who tended to be leaders and put them in charge of managing certain classroom activities. Students who were low performing, academic or behavior-wise, I often placed in charge of carrying out other classroom duties and they always tended to be the best at handling these types of jobs. By empowering students and placing them in charge I put them in a position to make their own decisions. I believe that police need empowerment as well.

Each year since 1998 the International Association of Chiefs of Police Community Policing Committee has recognized the best practices of law enforcement agencies around the world.[108] The Madison City Police Department in Alabama was recognized for taking steps to empower their police officers.[109] Madison realized that officers needed the ability to make decisions in real time without having to consult a chain of command.[110] Therefore, the department created a policy that empowered police and gave them the ability to act at the front-line level.[111] The policy only requires officers to ask themselves five questions before making a decision on their own: (1) Is the decision right for the citizens of Madison? (2) Is it right for the Madison Police Department? (3) Is it ethical and legal? (4) Are you willing to be accountable for your decisions? (5) Is it consistent with the Policies of the Madison Police

---

[108] International Association of Chiefs of Police, Community Policing Committee, http://www.iacpcommunitypolicing.org/about (last visited Mar 10, 2017).

[109] International Association of Chiefs of Police, Community Policing Committee, COMMUNITY POLICING BEGINS WITH EMPOWERMENT, http://www.iacpcommunitypolicing.org/profile?uid=185&blog=124 (last visited Mar 10, 2017).

[110] *Id.*

[111] *Id.*

Department?[112] If the answer to these questions is "yes", then officers do not have to ask permission to do what they believe is necessary in a situation.[113] For Madison, empowering officers in this way has lead to a decrease in complaints and an increase in citizen support.[114]

In the U.S., different police departments have different rules and training mechanisms.[115] Therefore, in an effort to create a more unified police force across state lines in regards to theory and practice, I propose law enforcement agencies everywhere combine and adopt the seven principles discussed in this paper: (1) establishing a consistent discipline policy, (2) allowing the creative learning process to take place through play, (3) providing a multicultural education, (4) creating and maintaining a respectable environment, (5) giving the utmost attention and support, (6) having high expectations, and (7) empowering police officers, in an effort to create a new and improved police force. Before police can handle one more person with a mental or physical illness as a well-abled individual[116][117], I propose they receive special guidance on how to work with this unique group of people by receiving a multicultural education. Before we have one more police officer go into a community and deal with a different group of people in a different area outside of the one he/she identifies with[118], they should be exposed to an education that

---

[112] Id.

[113] Id.

[114] Id.

[115] Telephone Conversation with Representative from Police Training Academy, (2017).

[116] UrbanWarfareChannel, POLICE BRUTALITY – COPS SLAM DISABLED BLIND MAN TO THE GROUND, YouTube (Mar. 11, 2017), https://www.youtube.com/watch?v=iM9sDdPED-M.

[117] David M. Perry, Justice for Down Syndrome Man Who Died in Movie Theater, August 29, 2013, http://www.cnn.com/2013/08/29/opinion/perry-down-syndrome-death/ (last visited Mar 11, 2017).

[118] John Eligon & Kay Nolan, In Milwaukee, Worries Over Eliminating Rule That Police Must Live in City, New York Times, August 19, 2016, https://www.nytimes.com/2016/08/19/us/when-police-dont-live-in-the-city-they-serve.html (last visited Mar 11, 2017).

allows them to understand and connect with the lives of those they serve.

In conjunction with these seven principles or techniques, I will now share an even deeper sentiment. It lies at the heart of our American criminal justice system; in the legislative and judicial branches of government. It would be irresponsible not to include the branches of government in the quest to better the nation's police force. Our judges and legislators, regardless of election or appointment, are key individuals in the process due to their position on the front lines of establishing police law and ensuring the carrying out of discipline for police when they fail to abide by them.[119] If these branches of government fail to provide justice for police misconduct then, as a society, we have little to no recourse.[120] We must not forget the important roles these persons play in our lives and the decisions they often make privately, which mean the difference between civil strife and unrest,[121] especially when riots can follow their decisions.[122]

VI. INVESTING IN NEW TRAINING TECHNIQUES AND PRINCIPLES

For individuals who believe we cannot afford or invest in a type of training that combines the seven principles outlined in this proposal…this type of training that looks into the psyche and emotional well-being of officers, then my answer is that we cannot afford *not* to have this type of police training. Every time we do not provide police with the skills, training, and resources they need we have more casualties, which includes police fatalities. According to a preliminary report

---

[119] Cynthia H. Conti-Cook, *Defending the Public: Police Accountability in the Courtroom*, 46 Seton Hall L. Rev. 1063-1065 (2016), *available at* http://scholarship.shu.edu/cgi/viewcontent.cgi?article=1573&context=shlr.
[120] *Id.*
[121] Rodney King, https://en.wikipedia.org/w/index.php?title=Rodney_King&oldid=769784000 (last visited Mar. 11, 2017).
[122] *Id.*

from the National Law Enforcement Officers Memorial Fund, the overall number of police

fatalities rose by 10% in 2016 and included officers killed in firearm-related incidents and

ambush attacks.[123] We also have more lawsuits settled outside of court with families of victims

of police brutality to the public's expense.[124] Between 2005 and 2015 the City of Boston paid

$36 million to resolve more than 2,000 legal claims and lawsuits against the Boston Police

Department.[125] Between 2004 and 2014 the City of Chicago paid $521 million in

brutality-related lawsuits.[126] Between 2004 and 2014 the City of Cleveland paid $8.2 million to

resolve lawsuits against police alleging brutality.[127] Between 2011 and 2014 the City of Dallas

paid out $6.6 million in substantial settlements and jury judgments. In one of the settlements

approved for $1.1 million, an African-American man was beaten and jailed on a charge that was

later dropped when video surfaced contradicting the officer's statements. The list continues: the

City of Denver, $12 million since 2011; Los Angeles, $101 million between 2002 and 2011;

Minneapolis, $9.3 million between 2011 and 2014; New York City, $348 million between 2006

and 2011; Oakland, $74 million between 1990 and 2014; and Philadelphia, $40 million between

2009 and 2014.[128]

When officers are not trained thoroughly before being placed on the streets to deal with

---

[123] Camila Domonoske, *Number of Police Officers Killed by Firearms Rose in 2016, Study Finds* (Dec. 30, 2016, 10:10 AM), http://www.npr.org/sections/thetwo-way/2016/12/30/507536360/number-of-police-officers-killed-by-firearms-rose-in-2016-study-finds.

[124] Nick Wing, *We Pay A Shocking Amount For Police Misconduct, And Cops Want Us To Accept It. We Shouldn't.,* http://www.huffingtonpost.com/2015/05/29/police-misconduct-settlements_n_7423386.html (last visited Mar 11, 2017).

[125] *Id.*

[126] *Id.*

[127] *Id.*

[128] *Id.*

citizens and their issues it can be dangerous. In addition to the above costs, we end up with more hurting families and more negative attitudes toward police. Studies have shown that direct contact with police is not necessarily enough to change attitudes toward police, but vicarious experience is key (i.e. learning that someone else has had a good or bad encounter with the police) in shaping a person's view of police.[129] A person's initial attitude concerning police plays a significant role in shaping how things turn out for them.[130] This is why we must invest in community policing as it helps to establish and build positive relationships with community members.[131] While in training, police should learn that doing their jobs is never a one way street.[132] Police are heavily dependent on citizens' cooperation and support to achieve success in their duties and performance.[133] Police must understand the public's trust and confidence in them is the cornerstone for cooperation and the basis for police legitimacy.[134]

Police should also be aware that local and national surveys have documented a constant race divide in attitudes toward the police, with European-Americans having more confidence in the police than African-Americans and Hispanics.[135] The question we must ask ourselves is why. In 2001, 2,500 randomly selected Chicago residents were interviewed as part of a citywide

---

[129] Dennis P. Rosenbaum et al., *Attitudes Toward the Police: The Effects of Direct and Vicarious Experience*, 8 POLICE QUARTERLY 343-365, https://www.researchgate.net/profile/Dennis_Rosenbaum/publication/258180173_Attitudes_Toward_the_Police_The_Effects_of_Direct_and_Vicarious_Experience/links/54be53130cf218d4a16a5a32.pdf (last visited Mar 11, 2017).
[130] *Id.*
[131] Stoughton, *supra.*
[132] Rosenbaum, *supra* at 343-344.
[133] *Id.*
[134] *Id.*
[135] *Id.*

evaluation of community policing.[136] The results confirmed the hypothesis that negative

experiences are associated with negative perceptions of police, while positive experiences are

associated with less negative perceptions of the police.[137] In short, if attitudes of citizens can be

changed and improved toward police and vice versa through such things as education and

community policing, then outcomes and experiences between police and citizens may change for

the better as well.

VII. REMEMBERING KING AND THE DREAM

In August of 1963, Dr. Martin Luther King would deliver the historical and famed *I Have

a Dream Speech.* However, prior to the speech, there were several events leading up to it that

reflect a tumultuous year regarding race relations and police brutality.[138] In April of that same

year, the body of William L. Moore, a Caucasian member of the Congress of Racial Equality,

was killed while on a one-man rights march to Mississippi to beseech the state's governor to

support integration efforts.[139] In the following month, more than 700 African-American youth

protesting in Birmingham, Alabama against segregation were clubbed by police, blasted with fire

hoses, and attacked by police dogs.[140] In June of 1963, Fannie Lou Hamer, an African-American

woman, was returning from a voter registration workshop with other civil rights activists when

she was arrested and later beaten so badly at the hands of police that she lost vision in one of her

---

[136] Rosenbaum, *supra* at 348
[137] Rosenbaum, *supra* at 354
[138] Equal Justice Initiative: A History of Racial Injustice (1995), http://racialinjustice.eji.org/timeline/ (last visited Mar 12, 2017).
[139] *Id.*
[140] *Id.*

eyes and suffered permanent kidney damage.[141] Her injuries contributed to her death in 1977 at the age of 59.[142] Just ten days later Medgar Wiley Evers, field secretary for the National Association for the Advancement of Colored People, was assassinated the same evening U.S. President John F. Kennedy gave his national speech outlining federal civil rights legislation.[143] In the first two weeks of August 1963, thirty-two teenaged protesters were jailed by police for protesting the segregation of public education.[144] Although unfortunate, these events set the stage for Dr. King's speech; a much needed address that would be remembered for years to come. A survey conducted in 1999 by researchers at the University of Wisconsin-Madison and Texas A&M University, of 137 leading scholars of public address, named Dr. King's speech as the greatest speech of the 20th century.[145] On August 28, 1963, Dr. King specifically addressed police brutality in his speech.[146] As Dr. King stood on a stage before 250,000 people from all over the nation, including celebrities and political figures[147], he stated that society could never be satisfied as long as the Negro was the victim of the unspeakable horrors of police brutality.[148]

This paper concerns police brutality, its origins in the United States, and suggestions for what can be done to counter it for good. Seven principles and techniques were introduced that,

---

[141] *Id.*

[142] *Id.*

[143] *Id.*

[144] *Id.*

[145] Gary Younge, MARTIN LUTHER KING: THE STORY BEHIND HIS 'I HAVE A DREAM' SPEECH THE GUARDIAN, https://www.theguardian.com/world/2013/aug/09/martin-luther-king-dream-speech-history (last visited Mar 12, 2017).

[146] Martin Luther King, Jr., I HAVE A DREAM SPEECH, STANFORD UNIVERSITY MARTIN LUTHER KING, JR. RESEARCH AND EDUCATION INSTITUTE, https://kinginstitute.stanford.edu/king-papers/documents/i-have-dream-address-delivered-march-washington-jobs-and-freedom (last visited Mar 11, 2017).

[147] Younge, *supra.*

[148] King, *supra.*

when combined, will yield a better police force just as doing so improved my classroom. And if I may add to Dr. King's statement…we, as a people, can never be satisfied as long as the Black, the White, the Christian, the Muslim, the Immigrant, the Native, the Straight, the Gay, those with accessibility issues or not, continue to be victims of the unspeakable horrors of discrimination from any group of people, but especially from those whom we hold to the highest esteem in our communities and from those whom we depend on to keep societal order: Our Police. The composition of our country is changing dramatically and rapidly.[149] It is not composed of just one race or one religion or one people.[150] Therefore, it is absolutely necessary that we employ a more thorough form of police training. The police deserve it. As a community, we deserve it.

---

[149] Gay, *supra.*
[150] *Id.*